REDEEMING THE TIME

Short Prayers from the Orthodox Tradition

✝ The initial inspiration for this little work was an ancient series of short prayers "written down by Saint John Chrysostom". A closer look revealed a hidden depth, as it were the description of the inner struggle towards a life entirely guided by the will of God. Inspired by this teaching from the Saint, the prayers are presented one by one, to aid our concentration when pondering Saint John's "Little Ladder" of good thoughts.

Given the difficulties of our times, especially such short prayers can be a great help: Easy to remember and needing little time, they can be used in almost any situation. But the importance of such humble prayers was brought home in unprecedented ways, when suddenly, all over the world, people were confined to their homes, unable even to go to church – an indispensable part of the traditional Christian effort, and even more so in times of need. Thus, as we were entering "the years of the great patience", we ended up with this little collection of short prayers, to inspire and encourage us towards living prayerfully wherever we may be: An aid towards "redeeming the time" (Eph.5:16, Col.4:5) – each according to our measure, and remembering that even great journeys are made by taking little steps, one at a time.

— With love in ICXC, *A

REDEEMING THE TIME

Short Prayers from the Orthodox Tradition

With Small Ponderings, Advice from the Saints, and a Simple Service with the Prayer of the Name

REDEEMING THE TIME, SHORT PRAYERS
FROM THE ORTHODOX TRADITION:
With Small Ponderings, Advice from the Saints,
and a Simple Service with the Prayer of the Name

+ + +

A first publication in the Series "Good Thoughts"
published by: Maranatha House (.info)
© AD 2023, A. Arnold-Lyklema

ISBN 978-0-9931058-7-6
CATEGORY: PRAYER & SPIRITUAL LIFE
INSPIRATION FROM THE ORTHODOX CHRISTIAN TRADITION

Table of Contents
with Introductory Notes

Short Prayer to the Holy Trinity
by St Ioannicius the Great   p.8

The first prayer in this little collection, a surprisingly short text from Small Compline, is both prayer and encouragement, an expression of trust in God as well as a confession of faith, glorifying the Holy Trinity in the joy of divine grace. It was written by a man who only later in life came to appreciate the Orthodox Christian vision, inspired by his meeting with a certain holy Elder, and eventually withdrew from the world to dedicate himself entirely to prayer. He reposed in the Lord at about ninety-four years of age, having grown great in virtue by the gift of God's grace. His service is found in the Menaion on the 4th of November.

A Little Ladder of 24 Prayers
by St John Chryostom
- A Little Ladder   p.10
- The 24 prayers, one by one   12
- The entire series of 24 prayers   62

The initial inspiration for this publication, this prayer is in itself a collection of short prayers – here presented one by one, so as to aid our concentration on the riches contained in each of these holy thoughts. Preceded by a general introduction on its character as "a little ladder" on the spiritual path, and with a small pondering next to each prayer. The entire series of twenty-four prayers is given once more at the end of this section.

The Prayer of the Name

- Notes from the Orthodox Tradition p.64
- The Prayer in practice 69
- Wisdom from the Saints 71
- Towards an Inspiring Prayer Rule 72
- The Prayer (basic text) 83

The Orthodox way of life has always been handed on in personal contact, and in the context of a living community. Similarly, the short prayers and small prayer service given here, simple as they are, were originally handed on against the background of the life of a traditional Orthodox Christian community – that is, the life of the Church in practice – including all the unspoken basics of vision, attitude, and way of life, which one normally learns simpy by growing up in such an environment.

However, in many parts of the world nowadays, Orthodox Christians may be living far apart, possibly just about able to attend the main church services for Sundays and the greater Feasts. In such a setting, the day-to-day Orthodox context is basically confined to one's own home – whilst anyone wishing to explore this Tradition any further may have to learn much from books and other written sources, rather than absorbing the Orthodox way in living contact with others on this path.

Nothing can replace direct personal contact, even more so in the spiritual life. Given the situation, however, it seemed helpful to accompany this little collection with at least some introduction into the basic Orthodox usage of the Prayer and similar short prayers, as well as on personal prayer in general – so that our own steps on this path, be they but small and humble, may be firmly rooted in the ancient but living tradition of the Saints.

As an Orthodox Christian writer once noted, the aim of such introductions is to present, as faithfully as possible, the ancient Christian wisdom, "not mine. I hope not to say anything original. If I do, ignore it." (Cf. "The Illumined Heart", a small book worth reading for its accessible and inspiring presentation of the Orthodox Christian teaching on how we can truly live in Christ. Publication details in the References)

To Remain Prayerful at All Times
- Advice in lockdown AD 2020,
  entering the years of the great patience   p.84
- A related series of short prayers   95

This series of prayers was proposed to the faithful as an aid for living prayerfully in these difficult times – here presented together with the accompanying advice.

The Breastplate
of St Patrick of Ireland
- An introduction, with some notes on the text   p.100
- St Patrick's prayer (core fragment)   102

The core fragment of St Patrick's famous prayer is a wonderful reminder of the life in Christ and the blessed protection of divine Grace, strengthened by the firm confession of the Mystery of the Holy Trinity.

References   p.104

Appendix: A Simple Service with the Prayer
- Introductory Notes   p.108
- Outline (for use with one's own prayer book)   110
- A Simple Service with the Prayer (full texts) 112

Inserted, a few pages with practical details:
- Common Prayer with the Prayer Rope:
  Basic Patterns & Alternatives   116
- Between the Rounds of the Prayer Rope   118
- The Basic Petitions and Intercessions (text)   120

✤

+ Some short prayers are very strong, combining the cry of the heart with a confession of faith in the Holy Trinity. One such prayer is known as the prayer of St Ioannicius, found in the service of Small Compline. The English rendering given here was inspired by that element of confession of our Faith. For more common English prose one could add the verb in the first line:

"The Father [is] my hope, the Son my refuge, the Holy Spirit my protection. O Holy Trinity, glory be to Thee."

The Father,
my hope

The Son,
my refuge

The Holy Spirit,
my protection

O Holy Trinity,
glory be
to Thee

A Little Ladder

Traditional Orthodox prayer books often include a series of twenty-four prayers by Saint John Chrysostom, which may have puzzled us by the additional inscription: "... according to the number of the twenty-four hours of day and night".

However, read attentively – one by one – these little prayers reveal a striking content: It is as if Saint John goes before us in the spiritual struggle, passing through all the ups and downs of the varying inner states, till finally arriving at the heartfelt wish to align himself completely with God's will, such that nothing in him would oppose the Divine Grace – so freely given despite all our shortcomings: Not like "buckling under" some inexplicably harsh discipline, but in the awareness that, truly, we could wish for nothing better than the will of our loving God "in Whom is no darkness at all" (1 Jn. 1:5).

Originally, these prayers may have been used like Orthodox Christians might use the Prayer of the Name, repeating them at least a few times at the change of every hour. Or maybe even more often returning to that one "thought for the hour", as a way to keep ourselves directed to the one thing needful.

But when we find ourselves unable to follow such a program – let alone at all hours "of day and night" – why not simply concentrate on one prayer at a time? Never mind how long it would take to complete the entire series.

When we realize our own weakness, as well as the fact that nowadays the world around us seldom aids us towards prayer, we can still be inspired by the prayers of the Saints: Each of us finding his or her personal measure – even if we choose just one little prayer a day, repeating it a few times to engrave its holy thought in ourselves.

The following pages were composed as an aid in such prayerful study of St John's "Little Ladder", presenting each prayer on its own double page. Short commentaries serve as a little introduction to the riches contained in these words – though, of course, you are very welcome to skip the commentary and simply ponder on the words of the Saint himself. At the end of this little series, all twenty-four prayers are listed together in the usual way, for easy reference.

Wishing you a blessed journey, through the prayers of St John Chrysostom and all the Saints,

+ M/p'a. Anke

Three Holy Hierarchs: Basil the Great,
John Chrysostom, and Gregory the Theologian

+ The Elder said: "Before all else ... pray, for without prayer no other good work whatever can be accomplished. ..... the perfection of prayer does not lie within our power, as the Apostle Paul says, "For we know not what we should pray for as we ought" (Rom.8:26). Consequently, it is just to pray often, to pray always, which falls within our power as the means of attaining purity of prayer, which is the mother of all spiritual blessings. Learn first to aquire the power of prayer and you will easily practice all the other virtues."

Εὐχαὶ κατὰ τὸ μέτρον
τῶν εἰκοσιτεσσάρων
ὡρῶν τοῦ νυχθημέρου
ἐπιγραφόμεναι
Ἰωάννῃ τῷ Χρυσοστόμῳ

PRAYERS

according to the number of
the 24 hours of day and night

written down by

Saint John Chrysostom

+ All our endeavours in this fallen world come to an end. And when death strikes, or disasters hit, all things seem so temporary, so fleeting. Truly, only that which goes beyond this life will remain: that which is eternal, heavenly. Thus, even the most negative experience becomes an invitation to redirect our life – our attention, time and efforts – as much as we possibly can; in such a way that, whatever happens, our intellect, our heart, and our whole being might be filled – even here and now – with God's eternal Grace.

O Lord,
deprive me not
of thy heavenly
and
eternal goods

+ The trouble is, that we do not even manage to stick to the good things we already know. We get distracted – by thoughts and worries, by all that goes on around us, by major events in the world, or just by all those little daily cares. We know that God is merciful. But when – in contrast with His infinite Love – we see the littleness of our life, and how we repeatedly fail to concentrate on the one thing needful, we come to realize the urgency of this cry of the Saints – that we may not live the torment of "too late".

*O Lord,
deliver me
from eternal
torments*

2

+ Saint Ignatius Brianchaninov wrote: "Books that have been left a long time unread in cabinets become filled with dust and can be eaten away by moths. If someone tries to read such a book, he finds it quite difficult to make out the words. This is my conscience. ... Only my grievous sins are clearly written. The smaller sins, which are very many, have been almost completely effaced ... I can hardly make out what was written." Mindful that we can even do harm with a well-meant but unwise word, our repentance begins to include all that we have forgotten, or maybe didn't even see.

O Lord,
if I have sinned,
be it in word
or in deed
or in my intellect
and reason,
forgive me

+ Even great Saints prayed God that He would not allow them to suffer utter poverty, so they would not be led to sin from human weakness and fear, denying His love. But praying thus for our daily needs, we begin to realize how ignorant we are of God's all-good will, and how forgetful we are of what we have already seen and received of Him. Seeing how ignorance and forgetfulness of Him make us sink ever deeper into spiritual sloth, till we become utterly insensible in heart and soul, our prayer becomes a cry to be delivered from all that leads us to sin, especially inside us.

O Lord, deliver me
from every need
and from ignorance
and forgetfulness
and sloth
and from
the stony hardness
of insensibility

+ Having come to see our own sin and spiritual poverty, we also begin to realize that we do not just sin of our own accord – we are indeed tempted: We get confused by thoughts; we are attracted to what is offered to us by the world around us. And we see how weak we are under the endless assault of temptations: We just cannot do it alone! But our withdrawing from God inevitably deprives us of the riches of His grace, so we cry for His help like a little child, longing for the warm comfort of His presence.

O Lord, deliver me
from
every temptation
and from
godforsakenness

+ "The sorrow of the world produces death" (2 Cor.7) and Saint Gregory Palamas comments, "If the soul's true life is the divine light conferred ... through spiritual grief, then the death of the soul is an evil darkness induced in the soul through worldly sorrowfulness." Who would not sorrow, when deprived of what he desires? Thus, whoever has tasted a little of God's grace may come to spiritual sorrow, when he sees himself desiring the world – which darkens our spiritual eyes and makes us forgetful of the things on High. Hence the ascetic's prayer: "O Lord, enlighten my darkness".

*O Lord, enlighten
my heart
which evil desire
has darkened*

+ Perhaps unexpectedly, in the ascetic Fathers the fruit of ongoing enlightenment in prayer, is their fundamental awareness of being human and living after the Fall. We are limited, mortal, and therefore all too easily inclined to fall into sin, despite our calling to become godlike: holy, perfect, and merciful, like our Heavenly Father (cf. 1Pt.1, Mt.5, Lk.6). But they also come to know God's infinite love and mercy with such certainty, that they overcome all despairing thoughts, crying in trust, "Have mercy on me".

O Lord, I sin,
being human,
but Thou,
being God,
have mercy
on me

+ When we are discouraged by the realization how we keep falling short of God's commandments, it is time simply to acknowledge our weakness. For only with God's help – in the fulness of His grace – will we be able to live up to our high calling. The "one thing needful" therefore, is to try and remain at all times close to our Lord and God – by prayer and psalmody, by reading His word, by keeping our mind on Him. Not aiming for any achievement of our own, but for the glory of Him who is the Source of all true blessings.

O Lord, see
the weakness
of my soul
and send down
thy Grace
to help me,
that in me
thy holy Name
be glorified

+ When Moses asked for God's Name, he learned that God is the One Who IS – "I AM THAT I AM" – the Source and Foundation of all being. And when the Son of God became incarnate, by divine command He was called "JESUS: for He shall save his people from their sins". This is the "Name above every name", given to us as the One Source of true salvation: That is, to be restored to the true life that is in Him, our Lord and God. Thus we pray in His Name, that we may live in Him till our very end, and be partakers of His Life for all eternity. (cf. Ex.3, Mt.1, Php.2, Acts 4, Jn.16)

O Lord Jesus Christ,
inscribe the name
of thy servant
in the book of life,
and grant me
a good end

+ In our efforts to be faithful to God, we easily get caught by the idea that we have to do something special to be accepted by Him. But what can we offer, other than what we have received from Him? All too often we do not even manage to be good stewards of the gifts we have received. And yet, the prophet proclaims His mercy, "Will a woman forget her child, so as not to have compassion upon the offspring of her womb? But even if a woman should forget these, yet I will not forget thee, saith the Lord." (Is.49)

O Lord my God,
I have done
nothing good,
but do not
take away
from me
thy compassion

+ In the poverty of our prayer, we may come to the point that all our spiritual life seems to be running dry. We know that we "have done nothing good", and we realize ever more deeply that we have no life in ourselves – we are created beings, with seemingly infinite possibilities but so infinitely poor when it comes to the fruit of the Spirit: love, joy, peace, longsuffering, kindness, goodness, faith, meekness, temperance (cf. Gal.5). Thus, even a tiny drop of His grace refreshes us – like the morning dew in the drought of summer.

O Lord, sprinkle
in my heart
the dew
of thy Grace

+ Whoever has tasted but a little of God's grace will long for an increase in that joyous and blessed life of the Spirit. However, when our prayerful efforts begin to cleanse our inner vision, we become sharply aware of the contrast between God's blessedness and our life in this world, falling so far short of the goodness of our Creator. And, realizing how even a bad thought adds to the burden of sin that weighs on the world, we join the cry of the Good Thief on the cross – having our hope only in His great mercy.

O Lord, God of heaven and earth,

I am sinful, shameful, wicked and defiled

- but according to thy great mercy, remember me,

when Thou comest into thy Kingdom

✛ One may be baptized as a child, or later in life at our own request – after which we are clothed in white as the symbol of our new life in Christ. Baptized, cleansed, and fragrant from the anointing which signed us with the Seal of the Gift of the Holy Spirit, we are called to remain in this blessed purity till the end of our lives. But we don't. Again and again we fall, and repent... and fall again. Thus we pray that God would not despise our feebleness but receive us again and keep us in His care, even though we do not deserve it.

O Lord,
receive me
in repentance
and
do not
forsake me

+ The prayers of the Church, found in the services as well as in the words of the saints, teach us the Christian life. We hear them, read them, pray with them... and thus we grow in understanding. However, with time we come to realize, paradoxically, how all this can be contained in a few words. The clearer we see things in God's light, the more our cry may be concentrated in the Prayer of the Name, or in the lines of the Lord's Prayer. Having realized our weakness and repeated falls, we simply beg our Lord – in godly fear – to keep us from temptation... not to betray His love.

O Lord,
lead me not
into
temptation

+ Based on their personal experience, the Holy Fathers teach us that every sin begins with some trace of a sinful thought – a first suggestion, whispered into our spiritual ears or presented to our inner eye, tempting us into the wrong direction. And they warn us that a city easily falls if there is no watch on the walls, and no gate-keeper to prevent evil from entering into the gates. Trying to keep our mind on God, and seeing ourselves incline to all sorts of thoughts, we pray for a thought well-pleasing to Him.

O Lord, give me a good thought

+ Elder Cleopa of Romania said, quoting St Basil the Great: "The greatest wisdom that guards a man from all sin, and guides him to perpetual happiness, is always to see death in front of you, and to have the Lord Jesus Christ in the intellect and heart (i.e. by the Prayer of the Name)." In this way, we truly come to see our sins, and learn to weep in heartfelt repentance – one of the most powerful spiritual means to cleanse our inner being. Becoming aware of God's forgiveness, we discover the unspeakable sweetness of "joyful mourning".

O Lord,
give me tears,
and the
remembrance
of death,
and that
sweet
compunction
of heart

+ Speaking of the Christian life, the Apostle wrote to the Corinthians: "For though we walk in the flesh, we do not war after the flesh – for the weapons of our warfare are not carnal, but mighty through God to the pulling down of strongholds: Casting down imaginations, and every high thing that exalts itself against the knowledge of God, and bringing into captivity every thought to the obedience of Christ" (2Cor.10:3-5) ... Such that every moment, every single thought, will lead the soul to dwell on the Beloved.

O Lord, give me
to redeem
my thoughts

+ Striving earnestly to "bring into captivity every thought", we cannot help seeing how far our world is removed from the Gospel of Christ. Nor can we escape the pull of this fallen world, if only because of the weakness of our earthly body. When Saint Anthony saw the snares of evil spread out over the whole world, he despaired how anyone could possibly overcome all this, and received the answer "Humility". But the path of holy obedience may be unexpected, as it was for St John the Baptist (above) when he baptized the Lord Himself.

O Lord,
give me humility,
and the
cutting away
of my fallen will,
and
holy obedience

+ In our struggle for true Christian virtue, all our personal difficulties – which we cannot avoid – become like "training ground" in the school of life. Father Alexander Yelchaninov wrote in his diary: "The conditions with which our Lord has surrounded us are the first stage leading to the Kingdom of Heaven..." And he stressed that all such conditions should be used as a path of salvation, a path towards a truly godly life: by converting "the bitterness of offenses, insults, sickness, labours, into the gold of patience, meekness, gentleness."

O Lord, give me
patience,
longsuffering,
and meekness

+ How can we remember and keep all God's commandments without fail, at every moment and in every encounter with others? A wise man, faced with a bad-mannered young prince, resolved the problem of "too many rules" by presenting the boy with one simple vision: To give heed to the royal person - to God's holy icon - hidden in everyone he would meet. However, for inner peace and godly patience we may need an even more fundamental truth: Not so much looking at ourselves or at other people, but living in the blessed fear of offending God's Presence, God's Goodness.

O Lord, plant in me
the root of
all that is good:
the fear of Thee

+ We have discovered the all-pervading influence of thoughts and imaginations; we have begged God for humility before Him; and for patience, longsuffering and meekness towards our brethren, and in all circumstances; and we have realized that we cannot live the Christian life unless we remain in the holy and blessed fear of God. Thus we return to the start of the path of Faith: our longing for God - wishing we could be fully given to that perfect love which wholeheartedly fulfills His Will - as the best and most blessed reality we could ever wish for.

O Lord, vouchsafe me
to love Thee

with all my soul,
and with all my mind,
and with all my heart,

and in all things
to keep thy will

+ In the joy of God's love we must not forget the warnings of the Prophets and Apostles: "If thou come to serve the Lord, prepare thy soul for temptation" and "All who want to live godly in Christ Jesus shall suffer persecution" (Sirach 2:1 & 2Tim.3:12). Thus, wishing evil to none, we pray for protection from all those who stand up against us, be they men or fallen angels. But at the same time, aware of our own fallen nature, we pray for protection from our own weakness – that we ourselves may not give in to the assault of temptations.

O Lord, shield me
from evil men
as well as
from demons
and the passions,
and from all
that should
never be done

✢ When, with the Apostle John, "we know that we are of God, and the whole world lies in wickedness" (1 Joh.5:19), we realize that not everything in this world is according to God's will – except for the fact that it is precisely His love which allows such freedom to His creatures... always seeking to invite them to the better path: "Thou desirest not the death of the sinner, but that he may return and live." Thus, even when suffering, we submit to His insight in ordering things for the best of each and all – simply seeking to remain within His will.

O Lord, as Thou
hast ordained
O Lord, as Thou
knowest
O Lord,
as Thou wilt:
let thy will
be done in me

+ Truly, the Resurrection is the key to the Christian life: The apparent defeat of the Cross of the Innocent Christ was turned into victory over death. Thus, all of us are invited to enter into that same way of life, with all the Saints: Accepting our calling, whatever the cost, in hope of God's final victory – trusting that His love and wisdom will lead the entire drama of Creation to the blessedness of His glorious Kingdom. And fervently we pray that indeed His will be done, and His Grace may shine in us, unhindered by our own fallen inclinations.

O Lord,
let thy will be done,
and not my fallen will.
Through the prayers
and intercessions
of the All-holy
Birthgiver of God,
and of
all thy Saints,
for blessed art Thou
unto the ages.
Amen

PRAYERS ACCORDING TO THE NUMBER OF THE TWENTY-FOUR HOURS OF DAY AND NIGHT

1. O Lord, deprive me not of thy heavenly and eternal goods.
2. O Lord, deliver me from eternal torments.
3. O Lord, if I have sinned, be it in word, or in deed, or in my intellect and reason, forgive me.
4. O Lord, deliver me from every need, and from ignorance, and forgetfulness, and sloth, and from the stony hardness of insensibility.
5. O Lord, deliver me from every temptation, and from godforsakenness.
6. O Lord, enlighten my heart, which evil desire has darkened.
7. O Lord, I sin, being human, but Thou, being God, have mercy on me.
8. O Lord, see the weakness of my soul, and send down thy Grace to help me, that in me thy holy Name be glorified.
9. O Lord Jesus Christ, inscribe the name of thy servant in the book of life, and grant me a good end.
10. O Lord my God, I have done nothing good, but do not take away from me thy compassion.
11. O Lord, sprinkle in my heart the dew of thy Grace.
12. O Lord, God of heaven and earth, I am sinful, shameful, wicked and defiled – but according to thy great mercy, remember me, when Thou comest into thy Kingdom.

13. O Lord, receive me in repentance and do not forsake me.
14. O Lord, lead me not into temptation.
15. O Lord, give me a good thought.
16. O Lord, give me tears, and the remembrance of death, and that sweet compunction of heart.
17. O Lord, give me to redeem my thoughts.
18. O Lord, give me humility, and the cutting away of my fallen will, and holy obedience.
19. O Lord, give me patience, longsuffering, and meekness.
20. O Lord, plant in me the root of all that is good: the fear of Thee.
21. O Lord, vouchsafe me to love Thee with all my soul, and with all my mind, and with all my heart, and in all things to keep thy will.
22. O Lord, shield me from evil men, as well as from demons, and the passions, and from all that should never be done.
23. O Lord, as Thou hast ordained; O Lord, as Thou knowest; O Lord, as Thou wilt: let thy will be done in me.
24. O Lord, let thy will be done and not my fallen will. Through the prayers and intercessions of the All-holy Birthgiver of God, and of all thy Saints, for blessed art Thou unto the ages. Amen.

The Prayer of the Name

NOTES FROM THE ORTHODOX TRADITION

Repetition is the mother of learning, as the old folk used to say. Likewise, the devout repetition of a single "word" (short phrase) is certainly not exclusive to the Orthodox Christian Tradition of the Prayer of the Name, also known as the Jesus Prayer, or simply "the Prayer".

However, just as the subject of our learning will determine what we learn by heart, even so is the Prayer unique on account of its content: Christian prayer is always addressed to another person: to the Personal, Triune God – or, by extension, to those close to Him.

In "The Ladder of Divine Ascent", Saint John Climacus relates how the ascetics in the desert would pray with one single thought, one "word" (often a short quote from the Bible) – as an aid to concentrate their whole being, and live their lives in a continous standing before God.

Eventually, taught by experience, the Fathers generally came to prefer the Prayer of the Name above other short prayers (though seldom exclusively). For those that love Him, there is a certain sweetness in that "Name above all names", like a foretaste of the life in Him.

In its practice this prayer is simple, concise, and clearly directed to the Son of God the Father: to our Lord and Saviour Jesus Christ – Whom none can truly call upon as "Lord" unless inspired by the Holy Spirit.

Whilst directing ourselves to Christ, we express our faith in the Holy Trinity, longing to become partakers of eternal life in the Triune God: "If a man love me, he will keep my words: and my Father will love him, and we will come unto him, and make our abode with him" (John 14:23).

Well known is the story of the Russian Pilgrim, who burned with longing to learn how one could possibly "Pray without ceasing" (1Thess.5:17) ... "since a man has to concern himself with other things also, in order to make a living." Unable to work it out by himself, he resolved to visit the churches and listen to "famous preachers", hoping to learn the answer from their sermons.

He relates, how he "heard a number of fine sermons on prayer; what prayer is, how much we need it, and what its fruits are, but no one said how one could succeed in prayer. [He] heard a sermon on spiritual prayer, and unceasing prayer, but how it was to be done was not pointed out."

Finally, he "settled on another plan – by God's help to look for some experienced and skilled person", someone who could teach him from personal experience. Eventually, he does indeed find a true Elder, who instructs him in a very practical way – for true prayer is learned in the practice of praying: "The continuous interior Prayer of Jesus is a constant uninterrupted calling upon the divine Name of Jesus with the lips, in the spirit, in the heart ... imploring His grace, during every occupation, at all times, in all places, even during sleep. The appeal is couched in these terms, 'Lord Jesus Christ, have mercy on me'."

The Elder explains how the concentration on this prayer eventually leads to such consolation that one can no longer live without it – to the point that the prayer will continue to voice itself within him of its own accord.

Such single-minded dedication to the Prayer really requires such an Elder as a guide – a true guide being a necessity for any journey into unknown territory, and even more so in the spiritual life. Nevertheless, all the faithful are encouraged to make use of it in all simplicity.

Elder Sophrony of Essex remarks how the Prayer is usually repeated without change. Nevertheless, he encourages us to adapt it to our changing needs, in order to remain alive to the reality of prayer: relating our entire life to Christ our God – as is done also in the series of prayers for the prayer rope proposed by the Bishop of Morphou (given in the next section, see p.84/95).

For only in that living relationship with our Creator, will we be able to accomplish our aim – as Christ Himself said, "I am the vine, ye are the branches: He that abides in Me, and I in him, the same brings forth much fruit: for without Me ye can do nothing." (John 15:5).

This is also what the Holy Elder explained to the Russian Pilgrim (an exerpt from this passage was quoted on p.12):

"Many people reason quite the wrong way round about prayer, thinking that good actions and all sorts of preliminary measures render us capable of prayer. But quite the reverse is the case, it is prayer which bears fruit in good works and all the virtues. Those who reason so, take, incorrectly, the fruits and the results of prayer for the means of attaining it, and this is to depreciate the power of prayer. And it is quite contrary to Holy Scripture, for the Apostle Paul says, 'I exhort therefore that first of all supplications be made...' (1 Tim.2:1). The first thing laid down in the Apostle's words about prayer is that the work of prayer comes above all else: 'I exhort therefore that first of all...' The Christian is bound to perform many good works, but before all else what he ought to do is to pray, for without prayer no other good work whatever can be accomplished."

A first taste of God's "great mercy" may come as a sudden gift, but the natural reaction to that is prayer. For "without prayer [man] cannot find the way to the Lord, he cannot understand the truth, he cannot crucify the flesh with its passions and lusts, his heart cannot be enlightened with the light of Christ, he cannot be savingly united to God. None of those things can be effected unless they are preceded by constant prayer. I say 'constant', for the perfection of prayer does not lie within our power, as the Apostle Paul says, 'For we know not what we should pray for as we ought' (Rom.8:26). Consequently, it is just to pray often, to pray always, which falls within our power as the means of attaining purity of prayer, which is the mother of all spiritual blessings. 'Capture the Mother, and she will bring you the children,' said Saint Isaac the Syrian. Learn first to aquire the power of prayer and you will easily practise all the other virtues. But those who know little of this from practical experience and the profoundest teachings of the Holy Fathers, have no clear knowledge of it and speak of it but little."

As to the dangers on the spiritual path, which some might warn against, all the Fathers point to one fundamental condition that is both the beginning, safeguard and result of the gift of God's grace: Humility.

Saint Silouan wrote, "Some there are who say that prayer beguiles. This is not so. A man is beguiled by listening to his own self, and not by prayer. Prayer is the best of all activities for the soul. Prayer is the path to God. By prayer we obtain humility, patience and every good gift. The man who speaks against prayer has manifestly never experienced the goodness of the Lord, and how greatly He loves us. No evil ever comes from God. All the Saints prayed without ceasing: they filled every moment with prayer.

"When the soul loses humility she loses grace and love for God at the same time, and ardent prayer is extinguished. But when the soul stills the passions and grows humble the Lord gives her His grace, and she then prays for her enemies as for herself, and sheds scalding tears in prayer for the world."

+ Seeking for true prayer, one would wish to pray with concentration and without hurry. A traditional aid towards this is the use of a prayer rope, usually made of wool, knotted in a particular way so as to make a circle of woollen beads – most commonly 100, 50, or 33 – closed with a cross from the same material (as, for example, in the photo on page 46). Having established how long it takes to pray one round, one can peacefully repeat the Prayer, moving one knot at a time, without further need to think about time or quantity.

THE PRAYER IN PRACTICE

As the Holy Fathers teach us, prayer is learned in practice, by exercising ourselves in prayer. Usually, our first experience of this comes from joining in with others – be it in the "little church" of the home, or in the Orthodox Liturgy and other church services. Those regular prayers "from the prayer book" or "according to the Typicon" teach us the language of prayer, as does the reading of the Psalms (in general, there is a deep resonance between the Orthodox church services and Holy Scripture). At the same time, all this – experienced in its proper setting – gives us a taste of what it is like to live in prayer.

When the Russian Piligrim began to practise the Jesus Prayer, under the guidance of his Elder, he was already accustomed to long church services that lasted for hours, as well as to reading many prayers at home – with lots of prostrations, as he himself recounts. Moreover, being free of cares, he had all the time of the world. Thus, with relatively little trouble, right from the beginning he spent nearly all his waking hours "working his prayer rope". But his was clearly an exceptional case.

In contrast, in our times, one busy man asked an Elder how he could possibly find time at all to say the Prayer – just a small round of thirty-three seemed too much already. In answer, the Elder proposed the following: "Surely, when you get up in the morning you have to dress and get yourself ready for work. Well, why not say the Prayer once, when putting on the one shoe, and then again when putting on the other. Finally, in this way having already made two bows, add a third for the sake of the Holy Trinity. Could you manage that?"

Of course, in no way could he protest the ease of that tiny "rule" of three Prayers, including the three small bows – but, having started like that, he quickly acquired a taste for the Prayer and gradually gave more and more time to it, till he longed to dedicate himself entirely to the spiritual life.

In these examples we see three or four distinct areas of prayer: First of all, the common services, at home (insofar possible with all the members of our household) and in church. Next to this, there is our personal "rule". Most often, personal prayer and the common "rule of the house" are arranged as a regular pattern of morning and evening prayers - possibly also including Bible readings.

Besides that, there is the effort – so zealously sought by the Pilgrim – to "pray without ceasing". As the Fathers teach us, exercising ourselves in the Jesus Prayer is one of the most effective ways to acquire the "habit" of prayer and keep a prayerful attitude throughout the whole day.

Nowadays many of us are struggling – like the busy man just mentioned – to keep up any sort of prayer rule. In this situation, many Elders have encouraged us to make use of the Jesus Prayer, as one of the simplest ways to start – easily learned by heart, and always available.

In addition, some ascetics from the Holy Mountain have shared with us how one may use the Prayer instead of the usual daily prayers and services – though the Liturgy itself, together with the Feasts and special occasions of the Liturgical year, remains irreplacable.

The general pattern for such a service, suitable for both common and personal prayer, is very simple: Opening Prayers, followed by Psalm 50 or 142, and the Creed. Then the Jesus Prayer (usually with some prayers to the Mother of God and the Saints, and possibly intercessions by name) – followed by some hymns, and the usual conclusion. To facilitate practical use of the above, further details are given in an appendix, including a few variations in common use.

WISDOM FROM THE SAINTS

The soul is sanctified and purified through the study of the words of the Fathers, through the memorization of the Psalms and of portions of Scripture, through the singing of hymns and through the repetition of the Jesus Prayer ...

That is, you can make a different kind of effort: to study and pray and have as your aim to advance in the love of God and of the Church.

Do not fight to expel the darkness from the chamber of your soul. Open a tiny aperture for light to enter, and the darkness will disappear...

+ Elder Porphyrios of Kavsokalyvia (+1991)

Keep your eyes blindfolded for just three days,
and afterward you will find
that the light of the sun hurts them.

Sever your bond with God for just three hours,
and you will find it painful to look at His light again.

You ask me, How long does my prayer last?
... I ceaselessly cense my faith with prayer,
lest the scents of the world blind it.

+ Bishop Nikolai Velimirovitch (+1956)

If I say one hundred prayers
in the silence of Mount Athos,
and you, in the noise of the city,
with work and family responsibilities,
say three prayers,
then we are in the same position.

+ Elder Efraim of Katounakia (+1998)

TOWARDS AN INSPIRING PRAYER RULE

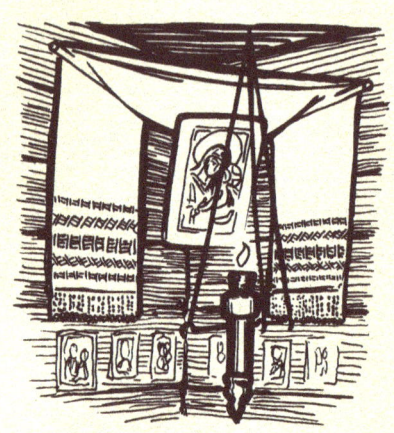

This little collection of short prayers is intended, first of all, as an aid and encouragement towards living prayerfully – wherever we are and in all simplicity – concentrating on the core of the Christian life, rather than presenting the entire Tradition in all possible details.

However, when using the Prayer (or similar short prayers) as part of our spiritual efforts, we inevitably meet with the question of measure: How much can we manage, and how do we keep that initial inspiration, day after day...

A time-honoured solution is to establish some sort of prayer rule, to help us to continue on the path of prayer despite the vicissitudes of life – that our intial zeal may neither slacken, nor burn itself out by taking on too much. On the other hand, when we can hardly manage to find time or energy for any kind of prayer, even the smallest rule may seem daunting – inspiring in principle, but so difficult to put into practice, given the present realities.

Traditionally, such perplexities would be answered in a personal relationship with a wise and experienced elder – based on trust and freedom rather than "discipline", and aimed towards truly living in Christ, even in the daily reality of our earthly life. Thus there is room for specific personal needs within the particulars of one's life and situation.

In such a context, a certain young person, full of questions about the inner life, wrote to St Theophan the Recluse (1815-1894) – a retired bishop who lived in ascetic seclusion but remained in correspondence with his spiritual children. In his answers, drawn from the wellspring of the ancient Christian Tradition, the Saint gives insight in the fundamental realities of the spiritual life, as a firm basis for one's own path, and as such, also more generally applicable.

The following notes, gleaned from some of these letters, are offered here simply as a collection of wise advice and possible patterns for a personal prayer rule – to be applied insofar as this may be helpful and inspiring. Saint Theophan was writing to someone already accustomed to a traditional prayer rule, and his words give us a glimpse of the vast extent of the Orthodox way of life and prayer. Against this background, he also provides some basic teaching on the use of the Prayer, even for people living "in the world".

(Besides prayer, our personal rule may also include spiritual reading, traditionally addressed as a distinct activity in its own right. One way, often found in combination with the prayer rule, is to follow the daily liturgical readings.)

Of course, personal guidance in the spiritual life remains invaluable, if only we could find such a person. This would not need to be a wonderworker or an elder of great fame, nor does such a person need to be a priest – for some it could simply be a wise older sister or brother in Christ (sometimes found in a monk or nun). Of crucial importance, however, is to find someone truly immersed in the prayers and wisdom of the ancient Church, and having fully made his/her own that world view – in some respects so different from the later Western understanding of the Christian path. (See the inspiring introduction, "The Illumined Heart", mentioned in the Introductory Notes. Details in the References, p.104).

With Prayerful Zeal

Remarkable is the great freedom with which the ancient ascetics used the established rules. Having been asked about a prayer rule, St Theophan recalls how "the greatest practitioners of prayer kept a prayer rule. They would always begin with established prayers..." – though when this inspired in them a particular prayer, they would abandon the set prayers and simply concentrate on that prayer. Thus, "if this is what the great practitioners of prayer did", it would be wise to follow their example and begin with a basic prayer rule.

Nevertheless, most important of all is to "maintain the heat of prayerful zeal" – wherefore it is "better to perform a small number of prayers properly", than to hurry through a long and impressive rule. To his young correspondent, St Theophan proposes, first of all, simply to follow the general practice of morning and evening prayers – making good use of the established prayers by reading them prayerfully. Later on, towards the end of the same letter, he introduces the use of short prayers as an alternative, which could even take the place of the entire rule (more about this later).

Assimilating the Established Prayers

As to what he calls "the established prayers", within the Orthodox Tradition we find two basic practices: Either using the service books (e.g. praying Small Compline in the evening) or making use of a standard collection of morning and evening prayers, gleaned from the prayers of the Saints and found in many Orthodox prayer books. St Theophan refers to this last practice, but his advice is equally applicable when using the service books, as he elaborates on the importance of entering into the meaning of the words, truly praying them "each time" with full attention.

He writes: "... spend a little of your free time at reading over all the prayers separately. Think them over and feel them, so that when you recite them at your prayer rule, you will know the holy thoughts and feelings that are contained in them." For prayer does not mean "just [to] recite prayers, but that we assimilate their content within ourselves" – saying them from the heart as our own prayer. Moreover, he encourages his young correspondent "after you have considered and felt the prayers" to learn them by heart. "Then you will not have to fumble about for your prayer book and light, when it is time to pray. ... You will see for yourself what a great help this is... [having] your prayer book with you at all times and in all places..."

Keeping the Mind on God

Whenever we come to stand at prayer, we should keep the mind from drifting, and not to let the heart grow cold and indifferent – making all efforts to remain attentive and prayerful. So as to make our prayer truly heartfelt, St Theophan suggests that we conclude our morning prayers by praying a little in our own words, "asking forgiveness for unintentional straying of the mind, and placing yourself in God's hand for the entire day."

Having thus made a good beginning, we are encouraged to "maintain prayerful attention to God throughout the day" – in order that our entire life may be lived in Him. In an earlier letter, St Theophan discussed living in continuous remembrance of God, by using all things we come across as a means to direct our thoughts to Him. Addressing prayer in particular, he mentions especially the use of short prayers as a wonderful aid to keep both mind and heart directed and concentrated.

"It is [also] good, very good, to memorize several psalms and recite them while you are working or between tasks.... one of the most ancient customs, mentioned by and included in the rules of St Pachomius and St Anthony." Suggesting a number of basic psalms from the divine services, the Saint encourages his young charge to memorize especially "the ones that strike your heart as you are reading them. Each person will find different psalms to be more effective for himself." Then, having memorized a number of Psalms, "you will always be fully armed with prayer. When some disturbing thought occurs, rush to fall down before the Lord with either a short prayer or one of the psalms..." – or a short prayer taken from the Psalms.

Having thus spent the day in prayerful striving, the time of the evening rule is our opportunity to be again more concentrated in our prayer to God. As in the morning, we may end in our own words, placing ourselves again in God's hands and, as the Saint puts it, "go to bed with a short prayer on your lips and fall asleep with it, or recite some psalm."

Concluding his words on the prayer rule, he stresses once more that all this is meant as an aid: "The most important thing" is to stand prayerfully before God, "with the mind in the heart" and whole-heartedly submitted to Him.

The Prayer Rope as an Alternative

With that aim in mind, St Theophan adds a few words on using the prayer rope (see further down for some practical details on how to do this) – either with the Jesus Prayer, or with some other short prayer, "expressing your need or giving praise and thanks to God." He explicitly stresses that this is not just for monks. "When you are praying with prayers that you have memorized and they do not move you, you may pray that day using the prayer rope, and do the memorized prayers another day. Thus, things will go better..." Even so, prayerful concentration does not come automatically: "Steadfastness and continuity of labour over oneself is an essential condition in the spiritual life" – although lasting peace of the thoughts is indeed a free gift from God, in answer to our earnest efforts in seeking His grace.

Prayer with Prostrations

An additional practice, perhaps unfamiliar to some, is the use of prostrations, as a physical means to help us to remain actively attentive at prayer. For their private rule with the prayer rope (often lengthy) some Fathers would sit down quietly, which may be equally advisable in cases of physical weakness. But the general Orthodox practice is to stand in prayer, literally – both in the church services and during our prayer rule – and from this position, bows from the waist and full prostrations can become a natural part of prayer. For those who are able, prostrations and bows – always combined with the sign of the cross (and getting up immediately in token of the resurrection) – are especially recommended during private prayer, as an aid to overcome the drifting of the mind and the general dispersion of our thoughts. This may be done according to need, when drifting off (standing up for this when seated) or, as St Theophan describes, one may make prostrations after each prayer from the prayer book, "as many as you like... accompanied by a prayer for any necessity that you feel, or by the usual short prayer."

Towards Prayerful Concentration

In another letter, speaking about attentiveness in prayer, St Theophan comments, "We undertake almost anything else, no matter how trivial, with some sort of preparation, but we set about prayer on the spur of the moment, and hurry to get through it as quickly as possible, as if it were... something extra, and not the most important thing of all. How then can we expect to collect our thoughts and feelings in prayer? ... Consider prayer as your first priority in life... Labour [at it]..." – and God will help. Once we begin to taste the sweetness of true prayer, it will "entice you toward prayer and inspire you to complete and attentive prayer."

In this context, the Saint also offers helpful advice in relation to our daily life and work, how to overcome "the disorderliness of our thoughts" as a result of our various occupations. First of all, the Saint points out that our daily occupations should not be considered as a separate part of our life, drawing us away from the life in God. Rather, we should do everything in the context of God's commandments – in a godly way and with the mind on God, thus remaining directed towards Him at all times.

Secondly, given that we do get distracted,, it is helpful to spend a little time preparing ourselves before we begin our prayer rule. St Theophan writes, "Do not stand at prayer immediately after household chores, conversations, or errands; instead, make some preparation for it, trying to collect your thoughts ahead of time and direct them toward standing worthily before God. Rouse within yourself the need for prayer at this particular time, because there may not be another time..." – realizing our deep and urgent need for Gods help, and remembering our aim: to find true rest in God.

Then (if we are able) we may begin our prayer rule by first making one or more prostrations, as a way to direct ourselves entirely to God from the start: "If misfortune threatens someone, and if he is standing before a person who can save him from it with a single nod of his head, is he going to stand there looking around? No, he is going to fall down on his knees before him and implore him. This is how you should be at prayer..."

Thirdly, St Theophan addresses the issue of worrying. Stressing that to perform each task with due care is simply one of our duties, he adds, "But worry, or the many worries that trouble the heart and give it no peace, is a disease of fallen man... try to drive it out and do not give it any ground. Have enthusiasm for your work and, performing it with utmost care, expect success from God [not from yourself], dedicating the task itself to Him, no matter how small it is, and you will get rid of worry." Thus we may do our everyday tasks without being distracted from God.

On Using the Prayer Rope

As for replacing the entire prayer rule with short prayers (even just simply, "Lord, have mercy") St Theophan offers some crucial advice on how to do this: "You should establish either a <u>number</u> of prayers, or a <u>time-limit</u> for prayer, or do both ... [For this reason, that] when we go about some outward activity, hours pass as if they were a minute. When we stand at prayer, however, hardly have a few minutes gone by, and it seems that we have been praying for an extremely long time. This thought does not cause harm when we perform prayer according to an established rule; but when somebody prays and is just making prostrations with short prayers, it presents a great temptation. This can put a halt to prayer that has barely begun, leaving the false assurance that it has been done properly. Thus, the good practitioners of prayer came up with prayer ropes, so that they would not be subject to this self-deception."

The prayer rope is "used as follows: Say 'Lord Jesus Christ, have mercy on me, a sinner,' and move one knot between your fingers. Repeat the prayer again and move another, and so on." Speaking to a young and ardent person, St Theophan also mentions the practice of combining the prayer rope with bows and prostrations, making "a prostration during each repetition of the prayer" (with the option to make smaller bows at each knot, and a full prostration at each of the marking beads, often included at intervals between the knots): "The prayer rule, then, is carried out in this way, standing and making bows."

Such physical efforts may not be suitable for everyone. Of crucial importance, however, is to establish a definite number of repetitions, establishing a time limit "so that you do not deceive yourself as to haste when you perform them."

First of all, one should work out the length of time available for the prayer rule (when replacing our usual rule,

already well established, we can simply note how long that normally takes us). "Then sit down, and see how many times you go around the prayer rope" within that set time-limit. Saint Theophan suggests doing this "not during your usual prayer time, but at some other time, although ... with the same attentiveness." Having established how many rounds we can pray unhurriedly within the given time, "let this quantity be the measure of your rule" – so we can simply pray, without worrying about the time or being fooled about the length of our prayer.

As mentioned before, one may alternate between this rule with the prayer rope and the prayer book, or replace our entire prayer rule with short prayers, using the prayer rope. At the end of his letter on prayer and the prayer rule, the Saint concludes, "I will repeat once again, that the essence of prayer is the lifting of mind and heart to God; these little rules are an aid. We cannot get by without them because of our weakness."

The Little Church of the Home

In the course of his teaching, St Theophan also remarked how good it is to pray in church, where "the prayerful spirit is quickly manifested, beause everything else there is directed towards that end". At home we may be aided in a similar way by arranging our own place accordingly – including the beautiful custom of the traditional icon-corner, often actually situated in a corner of the main room, sometimes also in everyone's personal bedroom: A special place to say our prayers... with one or more icons on the wall, lit by an iconlamp – like a little church.

Note: The Prayer of the Name may be shortened in various ways. The full text in Greek literally says "the sinner", but in English this may also be rendered as: "a sinner" (both versions are in use).

Lord Jesus Christ,
Son of God,
have mercy on me,
the sinner

Lord Jesus Christ,
Son of God,
have mercy on me

Lord Jesus Christ,
Son of God,
have mercy ...

To Remain Prayerful at All Times

Just before Lent AD 2020 the life of the Christian faithful was disturbed by the introduction of world-wide restrictions, imposed not just on those suffering from a flu-like infection (as might have been done in earlier times) but on the entire population. In a talk to his flock, Metropolitan Neophytos of Morphou (Cyprus) recounted the words of a holy ascetic in Cheesefare Week, that we were seeing "the last normal week" of this world.

In the weeks and months that followed, besides commenting on how to understand the various developments in all truth and with godly wisdom, several Hierarchs and Spiritual Fathers endeavoured to instruct the faithful how to continue the spiritual life in such unfavourable circumstances.

Measures varied from country to country, but the general advice from such holy men was to continue and intensify a life of prayer, as well as finding ways to partake of the Mysteries of the Church whenever possible, despite the awkward cirumstances: To pray, to confess, to attend the Church services, to partake of Holy Communion – these are basic necessities, essential to the life of the faithful, which cannot be replaced by online broadcasts.

In that respect, an example from ancient Greece springs to mind about a master painter, able to depict on a bare wall a fountain of water, or a delicous meal: However real those might look, he would be unable to quench his thirst or still his hunger. Similarly, the personal nature of our contact with both God and our neighbour naturally requires direct contact, unhampered by technical devices or imposed distance, and "with unveiled face" (2Cor.3:18).

Nevertheless, faced with severe limitations, our main efforts towards prayer – both personal and as a family – would be at home. Some commented that we were placed in a situation similar to the isolation sought by the holy hermits; however, for many this was involuntary, and without the preparation or fiery inspiration that brought those hermits to make such a choice.

In answer to this unusual predicament, we were presented with a rich treasure-house of advice on how to pray. Especially striking were the instructions from the Bishop of Morphou to his flock on how to deal with these unprecedented circumstances. Below are some exerpts from his words on that occasion, here offered in English translation for inspiration and encouragement – followed by a special set of short prayers, gleaned from his teaching.

INSTRUCTIONS FOR PRAYER, ADDRESSED TO THE FAITHFUL BY METROPOLITAN NEOPHYTOS OF MORPHOU

after the Presidential Announcement on 23 March AD 2020 (with new restrictions)

On the occasion of the new restrictions, introduced just before the Feast of the Annunciation, the bishop first instructed his flock in the local arrangements for the liturgical needs of the faithful (i.e. in his own diocese), since none of the general public would be allowed to come to church: The restrictions laid down by the state included keeping all church services 'behind closed doors', with only the priest(s), altar servant(s) and chanter(s).

After this, he offered the following teaching on how to deal with the situation, and how to exploit the accompanying involuntary isolation, so as not to be overcome by the spread of fear and panic, but to find spiritual benefit in this time of tribulation. (Translator's notes added in italics).

BELOVED CHILDREN IN THE LORD, in these circumstances, which God has allowed for our sins, let us keep in mind that all deaths, sorrowful tribulations, and pain, are NOT punishments – but opportunities for repentance.

And if we do not even grasp this opportunity
– to exploit it spiritually –
we punish ourselves with fear, panic, and insecurity.

As those before us used to say, with much wisdom (and let us remember, that to say such a word they used to fast for forty days): "Fear brings hell" – and "hell" *(Gk: kólasi)* means punishment.

And that fear, we humans bring upon ourselves – not the God of Love and of Righteousness!

Besides the above
(i.e. using this opportunity for repentance),
in order to acquire the gift of that perfect love which casts out fear,
as the Evangelist John the Theologian teaches us,

we fatherly propose to you, during this period in which you will all be confined at home, also to be prayerful.

In difficult, painful hours and moments, it is a great help to "tune in to the radio frequencies" of heaven.

Therefore, we propose to you:

To read daily the holy Psalter, i.e. the Psalms of David. These are psalms of repentance,
in which is hidden the Person of Christ, the Theanthropos.
(Theantropos: a patristic term – sometimes translated as "the God-man" – denoting the two natures united in the one person of Jesus Christ; who, as God incarnate, is both God and man.)

To read the lives of the saints,
especially of the contemporary saints,
of the 20th century,
whose lives are closer to our own life.

The life of a saint – to remind you of something which we have said at other times –
is a "gospel in practice" in our times.

We propose to you the lives of Saints Paisius, Porphyrius, Iakovos, Anthimus at Chios, Nicephorus the Leper, Eumenius Saridakis, George Karslides, Germanus of Stavrovouni, and other contemporary saints
– as well as, of course, more ancient saints.

It is also very helpful to read
(or to hear via the internet)
the Akathist or the Paraclesis to the Mother of God,
and to the Precious Cross.

Our diocese has also made available the Paraclesis to the Venerable Nicephorus the Leper, who seems to have been put forth by heaven – this great saint of our time – as an intercessor for all people who will flee to him for help.

Saint Nicephorus himself suffered painfully from a pestilent (infectious) illness – i.e. from leprosy – and found consolation, and meaning of life, and meaning of death, through the teaching of his elder, Saint Anthimos at Chios.

Now therefore, in his turn, Saint Nicephorus returns all those wonderful things, which he acquired through his pains and the cross of the pestilent illness of leprosy, to all of us – if only we ourselves, with humility, heartfelt pain, and faith, will seek his supplications.

HOWEVER, since the people of our times
have become used to quick ways,
without much effort,
we even propose – based on our little experience –
simply to say the following prayers:

> Great is the Name of the Holy Trinity!
> Most-holy Birthgiver of God, protect us.
>
> Lord Jesus Christ, have mercy upon us.
>
> All-holy Cross of Christ, save us by thy power.
>
> Great Archangel of the Lord, Michael, protect us.
> Great Archangel of the Lord, Gabriel, enlighten us.
>
> Saint of God, Nicephorus, pray to God for us.

Let each say these prayers, using his prayer rope.

If you have a prayer rope with thirty-three knots, thirty-three times. If you have one with fifty knots, fifty times. If you have one with a hundred knots, one hundred times. If you have a larger one, with three hundred knots, pray according to the time available to you

– you will now have at your disposition a lot of time;
let not yourselves be cheated
by all that is available on television and internet.
Give more time to the "network on High"!

Instead of the name of Saint Nicephorus – i.e. when we say "Saint of God, Nicephorus ..." – you can call upon the name of any other saint, as you desire.

Similarly, let us also pray for others,
for our fellow-men in the whole world:

> Lord Jesus Christ,
> have mercy upon thy servants (N.)

And we say their first names – of all those we know. After which we continue, as many times as we mentioned above (using our prayer rope), repeating simply:

> Lord Jesus Christ, have mercy upon thy servants.

Similarly, we say:

> Lord Jesus Christ,
> have mercy upon thy whole world.

Once, Saint Paisius told us that we may combine these two prayers, i.e. to say:

> Lord Jesus Christ, have mercy upon thy servants
> and upon thy whole world.

And, finally, for those who have fallen asleep – who are not dead at all, they have not really died; especially the righteous have found boldness and strength in the sight of the Triune God –

let us beseech them, as well as beseech the Lord for them, and not only for the righteous, but even more for those people for whom it is difficult in the light of the Triune God,

and let us pray to the Conqueror of death,
and say to Him:

> Lord Jesus Christ, give rest to thy servants (N.)

We start by saying their first names, and then we repeat the general prayer for their rest:

> Lord Jesus Christ, give rest to thy servants.

MY BELOVED, this trial is a great opportunity for us all, to open our heart and our soul in repentance and prayer. And, in that way, our Triune God shall cleanse us from both spiritual and bodily microbes.

And, to end with something lovely, which a person of God said to me: To uplift the soul, and for consolation in this involuntary seclusion – which may possibly lead quite a number of people to sorrow or depression –
it is good, besides the prayers that we have mentioned, to listen also to some traditional chant,
or even some greek folk-song. *(Transl.: For such traditional chant and folk-songs were rooted in the same Christan Faith and way of life, and thus revive in us the inspiration of our forefathers to continue in the way of Christ.)*

This is also a medicine for the soul, being part of our Greek (Orthodox Christian) identity. And it is not the bishop of Morphou who says this – who, as you know, is very fond of Greek folk-songs and Greek music. This was said to me by an ascetic woman, that I might hand it on to you.

AND DO NOT FORGET the prayer, which we have also mentioned elsewhere:

> My Christ,
> give me the patience and the faith of the Saints.

Now we have entered, as you will understand, the years of the great patience *[cf. Lk.21:19; Rev.3:10; 13:10; 14:12]*. And for that great patience, the faith of my grandfather and my grandmother does not suffice; that needs the faith of the Saints. And if we ask for that with heartfelt pain, Christ will liberally give it to us.

Thus, each family can elevate its own house to be a "church at home". For no difficulty can, and never should, separate us from Christ, from His grace and power.

And, to conclude,
the greatest problem, according to my humble view,
is not – in the present situation –
the spreading of the illness, as many have presented it,
causing the world to panic.

That problem does exist, BUT
the greater problem, ultimately,
is the fear, the panic,
and the limitless, unprofitable tele-watching.

There seems to be a deliberate intention,
from certain powers of "the new dis-order"
that people should be full of fear and panic,
and some – not all, of course – in the realms of television
are serving that purpose.

That fear and that "telemania" will not go away
through presidential orders,
nor through episcopal encyclicals like my own.

Those things – i.e. the fear, the panic, and the rest –
will begin to lessen, and in the end vanish altogether,
when we begin to repent
for our personal passions and faults,
and ask the Holy Spirit, with pain of heart:

> O Holy Spirit, Spirit of Truth,
> cleanse us from all defilement!

With many prayers and the love in Christ,

+ your Bishop, of Morphou.

FROM THE SAME, ON RECEIVING THE HOLY GIFTS AT HOME

Given the restrictions on church gatherings, in the diocese of Morphou arrangements were made, for any of the faithful who would desire it – in fear of God, in faith and love – to receive the Mysteries at home, especially Holy Communion. People could also ask to be brought Holy Unction, Holy Water, and Antidoron.

Besides, provision was made for the celebration of namedays, and for the services for the departed (in both cases, kolyva would be made in the priest's household and, after the service, taken to the appropriate homes).

Everyone was also invited to continue to give names for commemoration in the church services. (Any of these liturgical needs would be communicated by telephone or text-message to the priests, deacons, altar-servants or chanters of one's parish.)

At the end of his address to the faithful, given above, metropolitan Neophytos added a little word of instruction on receiving the Holy Gifts at home. In some regions, even this might not have been possible. Nevertheless, it seemed good to include his words, in case anyone in similar isolation might have this blessed opportunity:

THE ISOLATION of the majority of the faithful from the Divine Liturgy, and all the Holy Services, is very painful for all of us. However – whilst [various national and international decrees] keep the faithful far from the Body and Blood of Christ, of the humble Jesus – when our good priests and deacons are willing, the Holy Gifts can come to your house.

It suffices for you to prepare,
to forgive everyone from the depth of your heart,
and to pray as we have set out above.

"And the Master," as my grandmother Myrophora used to say, "comes even to the house of the humble."

– to the house where we dwell, and thereby also to the house of my humble soul, which is "entirely desolate and fallen in ruin," but "since Thou dost will to dwell in me, I dare to draw nigh."

And when higher powers prevent me to come to Thee, my Christ, then the humble Jesus, who became incarnate of the Holy Spirit and the Virgin Mary, accepts to come into our house, into our body, into our soul
– unto forgiveness of sins and unto life eternal.

GOOD STRENGTH!
And, God-willing, we shall speak again.

Through the prayers of our holy Fathers,
Lord Jesus Christ, our God,
have mercy upon us and save us.

To remain prayerful at all times,
using our prayer rope:

Great is the Name of the Holy Trinity!

Most-holy Birthgiver of God, protect us

✤

Lord Jesus Christ, have mercy upon us

All-holy Cross of Christ, save us by thy power

✤

Great Archangel of the Lord, Michael, protect us

Great Archangel of the Lord, Gabriel, enlighten us

✤

Saint of God, [Nicephorus], pray to God for us

For our fellow-men
in the whole world:

> *Lord Jesus Christ, have mercy
> upon thy servants (N.)*
>
> *Lord Jesus Christ, have mercy
> upon thy servants*
>
> *Lord Jesus Christ, have mercy
> upon thy whole world*
>
> *Lord Jesus Christ, have mercy
> upon thy servants
> and upon thy whole world*

And for those
who have fallen asleep:

> *Lord Jesus Christ, give rest
> to thy servants (N.)*
>
> *Lord Jesus Christ, give rest
> to thy servants*

Entering the years
of the great patience:

> My Christ,
> give me the patience
> and the faith
> of the Saints

In repentance for our
personal passions and faults:

> O Holy Spirit,
> Spirit of Truth,
>
> cleanse us
> from
> all defilement!

The Breastplate

The prayer of Saint Patrick, given on the following pages, is known as "The Breastplate" – that is, a piece of protective armour – wherewith he committed himself to the protection from on High.

It is the beloved conclusion of a longer prayer, which carries the same name, in which the Saint refers to the entire economy of Salvation and to all the glory of God's creation. In these last lines, however, his entire thought becomes fixed in God – desiring to be at one with Christ in every place and circumstance, confessing his firm faith in the Holy Trinity, and seeking all his protection in the presence of God's Grace.

Notes on the text:

The last lines, from "Salvation is of the Lord..." to the end, have been handed on in Latin (possibly reflecting the fact that this goes back to a biblical expression, which he himself might have received in Latin) whilst the rest of the prayer contained in the ancient manuscripts is in old Irish. There exist several versions in English, some more freely rendered and/or adapted to metre. Study of the manuscripts, by a number of scholars, has clarified the meaning of certain expressions, giving rise to alternative translations, some of which are worth noting here:

The lines in ancient Irish, rendered as "Christ where I lie down, Christ where I sit, Christ where I arise", were shown to contain a reference to Ephesians 3:18, and therefore

might also be translated: "Christ in (all) the breadth, Christ in (all) the length, Christ in (all) the height".

According to some scholars, the original Irish expression translated as "the Creator of all things" may also include a reference to God as the Judge of all.

The ancient Irish verb in "I arise today in a mighty strength" contains the root for "to join" and could also be translated "I bind to myself..." – that is, I put on a breastplate of great power, by prayerfully calling upon God the Holy Trinity.

Aside: As is well known, the humble three-leafed clover or trefoil, served Saint Patrick as an illustration of the Mystery of the Triune God, in Whom he so firmly trusted.

CHRIST with me,
Christ before me, Christ behind me,
Christ within me,

Christ beneath me, Christ above me,
Christ on my right, Christ on my left,

Christ where I lie down,
Christ where I sit,
Christ where I arise,

Christ in the heart
of everyone who thinks of me,

Christ in the mouth
of everyone who speaks to me,

Christ in every eye that sees me,
Christ in every ear that hears me.

I arise today
through a mighty strength,
calling upon the Trinity:

I believe in the Three,
and I confess the One,
the Creator of all things.

Salvation is of the Lord!

Salvation is of the Lord,
Salvation is of Christ.

May Thy salvation, O Lord,
ever be with us.

REFERENCES

Introductory Notes

"The Illumined Heart: Capture the Vibrant Faith of Ancient Christians", by Frederica Mathewes-Green. Publ.: Paraclete Press, 3rd paperback printing AD 2012 (1st printed in 2001).
ISBN 978-1-55725-553-2

Concerning the 24 Prayers from St John Chrysostom

ΜΕΓΑС ΚΑΙ ΙΕΡΟС СΥΝΕΚΔΗΜΟС ΟΡΘΟΔΟΞΟС ΧΡΙСΤΙΑΝΟΥ. Publ.: Papademetriou, Athens, edition AD 2015 (1st publ. 1954).

(Title page) From the words of the Elder to the Pilgrim, as related in "The Way of a Pilgrim" (Ch.1, p.7-8, 2nd edition 1952 / 3rd printing, paperback). Transl.: R. M. French. Publ.: Seabury Press, New York.

(3) "The Refuge – Anchoring the Soul in God" (ch.7, p.98) by St Ignatius Brianchaninov. Publ.: Holy Trinity Monastery, Jordanville, New York, AD 2019. ISBN 978-0-88465-429-2

(6) "To the Most Reverend Nun Xenia", a text by St Gregory Palamas, from the Philokalia. See the English edition "The Philokalia (Volume IV)" prepared by G.E.H. Palmer, Phillip Sherrard and Kallistos Ware.
Publ.: Faber and Faber, London, AD 1995.
ISBN-13: 978-0-571-19382-0 / ISBN-10: 0-571-19382-x

(16) Quoted from a small film in Romanian, with English subtitles, made during Elder Cleopa's lifetime (further details unknown).

(19) "A treasury of Russian Spirituality" (p.458). Edited by: G.P. Fedotov. Publ.: Sheed and Ward Ltd, London, 1977 (1st publ. 1950).

On the Jesus Prayer

"The Ladder of Divine Ascent", by Saint John Climacus. Available in various editions.

"The Way of a Pilgrim & The Pilgrim Continues his Way" (second edition, 1952 / third printing, paperback). Transl.: R. M. French.
Publ.: Seabury Press, New York.

"Wisdom from Mount Athos: The Writings of Staretz Silouan, 1866-1938" (Chapter "On Prayer", p.85). A first collection by Archimandrite Sophrony. Transl.: Rosemary Edmonds.
Publ.: Mowbrays, London & Oxford, 1974.

"On Prayer", by Elder Soprony (Sacharov) from Essex. Published by the Monastery of St John the Baptist, Tolleshunt Knights, Essex, UK.

"The Spiritual Life, and how to be attuned to it", by St Theophan the Recluse (esp. Ch.47 and 48-49). Transl.: Alexandra Dockham.
Publ.: St Herman of Alaska Brotherhood & St Paisius Abbey, AD 2000 (1st printed in 1995). ISBN: 0-938635-36-0

Details for services with the Prayer were received in the traditional way, by participation and/or in personal contact with others from "the household of the faith" (Gal.6:10).

About St. Patrick's Breastplate

Cf. Charles H. H. Wright (referring to the work of Dr. Whitley Stokes) in: "The Writings of St. Patrick", Christian Classics Series VI, 3rd edition.

Translations

Texts for prayers and hymns were gleaned from various sources, where possible checked against the original Greek, or sometimes newly translated. Due to the variety in English usage, in both style and terminology, a work like this inevitably requires choices (in a few common prayers indicated by square brackets). Hopefully these may be inspiring, but begging the reader's forgiveness for any awkward variations with what one may be used to.

On the Prayer to the Theotokos

Some of the traditional titles of the Most-holy Virgin come in varying translations. The original Greek text of the short prayer used with the prayer rope has "Theotokos" – the ancient title confirmed by the third Œcumenical Council, held at Ephesus in AD 431. Sometimes left untranslated, it may be translated as "Birthgiver of God". In some translations it is rendered as "Mother of God", although in Greek this is actually a different title for the Virgin Mary – in certain hymns both titles are used next to one another. To date, all three versions are widely used, besides the occasional descriptive rendering (e.g. "who brought forth God" or "who gave birth to God").

This title not only honours the Virgin Mary as such, but expresses the fact that Jesus Christ is truly God incarnate, "one in essence with the Father", as it says in the Creed. Thus, being God-and-Man, uniting both natures in Himself, He opened the way for us to be united with God.

Some are troubled by the actual prayer, asking the Theotokos to "save us". Indeed, Jesus Christ is the one and only Saviour. However, those united with Him become filled with divine Grace, and thus they themselves become instruments and even co-workers of God's Salvation – like an earthly coal glowing with divine fire, able to light up others also; or like a "'rusty tap" (as one holy elder called himself) gushing forth living water.

In some sense, every one of us is invited to become such a vessel of God's grace, like the multitude of saints gone before us. As it says in the Gospel (Jn. 14:23), "If a man love me, he will keep my words: and my Father will love him, and we will come unto him, and make our abode with him." However, the incarnation of the Son and Word of God was a truly new event in history, only to happen once. Thus the "Virgin Birthgiver of God" (or: Virgin Theotokos), as she is often called in Orthodox hymnography, has a special place and function among all mankind, as the one who bore our God and Saviour bodily, besides being filled with the Holy Spirit in a spiritual sense.

Therefore all generations magnify her as the precious and blessed vessel through whom our Lord, God and Saviour Jesus Christ came into the world to save mankind and, in the words of St Romanus, to open unto us the way "back to paradise". And, like we may ask for the prayers of people near to us, so do we ask the Mother of God, and all the Saints in heaven, to come to our aid – having learned, from human experience throughout the generations, of their Christ-like love for the faithful and for all mankind.

ILLUSTRATIONS

Some of the illlustrations in this little work are from our own hand, others were graciously given for use in our publications (including a number of drawings by Fr. John Matusiak) or else found in the public domain – here used with gratitude towards all those who have made their work available with such generosity, providing a rich treasury to choose from. Special mention is due for the drawing of the icon corner (on page 72) and the illustration on the last page, both created by Alvin Alexsi Currier and made available online by the Orthodox Arts Journal, as part of the Illustration Project. Wishing God's blessing on all the cheerful givers! *A

Appendix

A SIMPLE SERVICE WITH THE PRAYER
– INTRODUCTORY NOTES –

The use of the Prayer, as such, is deeply rooted in the ancient ascetic tradition of the Church. The continuing custom to use the Prayer instead of the usual daily services "according to the Typicon", originated in situations with limited possibilities to celebrate the full liturgical cycle – which, as such, is common to all Orthodox Churches anywhere in the world.

Ascetics from the Holy Mountain have handed on a basic pattern for such simple services with the Prayer. As is apparent from the various rules, so generously shared by those Elders for the benefit of the faithful, details like hymns and special petitions do vary, and may also be adjusted according to local needs and possibilities.

Needing few books and easily learned by heart, this service is suitable for both personal prayer and common prayer, for both small households and larger communities – allowing any of the faithful to join in with the prayer of the Church at all times.

Only the Divine Liturgy and other Mysteries can never be replaced in this way, nor the various special occasions related to the Feasts and Fasts of the liturgical year. For such services, therefore, the faithful have sometimes travelled long distances, even on foot, if necessary.

A Shorter Rule for All Situations

A shorter and very simple service may start with the Opening Prayers, the Psalm and the Creed, followed by the Prayer as much as desired (see p.117 for a few options). Then close with one or more Troparia, and the Dismissal.

If no books are present (e.g. when travelling) we may use the troparia we know by heart.

Multi-lingual Services

When the local language is not common to all those present, the basic framework is usually done in one or two languages understood by most, if not all – whilst those saying the prayer ropes to the Lord and the Theotokos may use their own native tongue. Thus the Prayer as such can be said wth one's whole being, whilst everyone can understand the service at least to some measure.

Liturgical Usage

In some communities this service is done in church, like any of the usual church services. All the set prayers (opening prayers, doxology, etc) are done in the usual way, as noted in the rubrics. If no Priest is present, we simply leave out his part, reciting the rest as usual, unless otherwise noted.

Included here are the basic rubrics for the Paschal season. With access to a church calendar and/or the appropriate service books, we can join the celebration of the liturgical year on a daily basis – in the prayers to the Saints, the Troparia, and the final blessing by the Priest.

Using This Book

The outline on the next pages can be used in combination with a regular Orthodox prayer book, which will normally include at least the basic prayers. In this way, one may do the service with texts in one's customary translation.

In case such a book is not readily available, the full text of prayers and hymns has been added as a separate chapter (p.112 ff). Thus, if necessary, one can do at least the basic service with simply a Bible or Psalter (and possibly a church calendar) besides this book.

The petitions to be said with the prayer rope are inserted at the appropriate place as a separate section, for easy reference – with a number of variations in common use, as received from various sources (see p.115-121).

OUTLINE FOR SERVICES WITH THE PRAYER

OPENING BLESSING, if there be a Priest: Blessed is our God... / Reader: Amen. Otherwise, the Reader begins: Through the prayers of our holy Fathers...

OPENING PRAYERS, as usual:
Glory to Thee, O God, glory to Thee. Followed by: O Heavenly King... And the Trisagion: Holy God... Then: Glory/Both now. All-Holy Trinity... And: Lord, have mercy (3x). Glory/Both now. And the Lord's Prayer: Our Father... Amen.

> NB: From Pascha till Pentecost, we do not recite "O Heavenly King" (nor the preceding "Glory"). Moreover, during the first 40 days, till the Leavetaking of Pascha, we replace the opening Trisagion ("Holy God..") with the Paschal hymn: Christ is risen from the dead, trampling down death by death, and upon those in the tombs bestowing life. (3x) – After which we continue as usual with "Glory/Both now... All-holy Trinity..." (etc).

AFTER THE LORD'S PRAYER:
Lord, have mercy. (12x) Glory/Both now. Then: O come, let us worship, OR (Paschal) Christ is risen..., see notes on p.113.

Then the PSALM:
In the evening, Ps.142 (143), O Lord, hear my prayer...
In the morning, Ps.50 (51), Have mercy on me, O God, according to thy great mercy...

After the Psalm, the Reader concludes: Glory/Both now.

Then the SYMBOL OF FAITH (the CREED): I believe... followed by the Prayer >> for details, see p.115-121.

After the last round of the prayer rope, concluded with "Glory/Both now. Alleluia...", we continue with one of the following, introduced in the usual way: 1) The GREAT DOXOLOGY – in some places only on the eve of the Liturgy and in the mornings; and instead, on all other evenings, 2) The

NINTH ODE (Lk. 1:46-55) with its refrain: **More honourable ...**

Then the TROPARIA, following the usual pattern (as in Daily Vespers or at the beginning of Matins) depending on the weekday and/or feasts and periods of the Liturgical year. Except on the Great Feasts, one may also add the apolytikion of the local church/chapel(s).

> Alternatively, instead of the troparia, we may chant to the Theotokos (as at the end of Vespers in a Sunday Vigil): **Rejoice, O Virgin...** (3x)
>
> BUT IN THE PASCHAL SEASON, instead of the troparia mentioned above, the Paschal Troparion: **Christ is risen from the dead...** (3x). Or else, if available, the appointed troparia from the Pentecostarion.

We conclude with the usual DISMISSAL, omitting the priestly exclamations if no Priest be present:

[Priest: **Most-holy Birthgiver of God...**]
Reader: **More honourable ...**

[Priest: **Glory to Thee, O Christ....**]
Reader: **Glory/Both now. Lord, have mercy.** (3x)
[and, if a Priest be present: **Father, give the blessing.**

Priest: **May .... Christ our true God ...** / Reader: **Amen.**]
[Or else, Reader: **Through the prayers of our holy Fathers, Lord Jesus Christ, our God, have mercy upon us. Amen.**]

At certain times, we add one FINAL HYMN. In the evening: **Under thy compassion.** Instead, on Wed/Fri (eve and morning) we may chant: **Before Thy Cross...** (3x). And then the Priest (or Reader) concludes with: **Through the prayers...**

BUT IN THE PASCHAL SEASON, after the blessing by the Priest "May..." (or: "Through the prayers", if without a Priest) we chant the Paschal ending as follows (or as in local usage):

– AND HE GAVE US LIFE ETERNAL,

LET US VENERATE HIS RESURRECTION ON THE THIRD DAY.

A SIMPLE SERVICE WITH THE PRAYER

If there be a Priest, he gives the Opening Blessing:
Blessed is our God, always, now and ever, and unto the ages of ages. / Reader: Amen.

Otherwise, the Reader begins:
Through the prayers of our holy Fathers, Lord Jesus Christ, our God, have mercy upon us. Amen.

Then the Opening Prayers:

Glory to Thee, O God, glory to Thee.

O HEAVENLY KING, Comforter, Spirit of Truth, Who art everywhere present and fillest all things; Treasury of good things, and Bestower of Life: Come and abide in us, and cleanse us from all defilement, and save our souls, O Thou who art Good.

TRISAGION: Holy God, Holy and Strong, Holy and Immortal, have mercy upon us. (3x)

NB: From Pascha till Pentecost, we do not recite "O Heavenly King" (nor the preceding "Glory"). Moreover, during the first 40 days, till the Leavetaking of Pascha, we replace the opening Trisagion ("Holy God..") with the Paschal hymn: Christ is risen from the dead, trampling down death by death, and upon those in the tombs bestowing life. (3x). After which we continue as usual with, Glory/Both now, etc – as set forth below:

Glory [be] to the Father,
and to the Son, and to the Holy Spirit,
both now and ever,
and unto the ages of ages. Amen.

ALL-HOLY TRINITY, have mercy on us. O Lord, blot out our sins. O Master, pardon our iniquities. O Holy One, visit and heal our infirmities, for thy name's sake.

Lord, have mercy. (3x)
And, as above,* Glory/Both now.

OUR FATHER, who art in the heavens, hallowed be thy name; thy kingdom come; thy will be done, on earth as it is in heaven. Give us this day our daily bread; and forgive us our debts, as we forgive our debtors; and lead us not into temptation, but deliver us from the evil one.

[Priest: For thine is the kingdom, the power, and the glory, of the Father, and of the Son, and of the Holy Spirit, now and ever, and unto the ages of ages.]

Reader: Amen.

Lord, have mercy. (12x)
Glory/Both now.

O come, let us worship God our King. O come, let us worship and fall down before Christ, our King and our God. O come, let us worship and fall down before Christ Himself, our King and our God.

[NB: During the Paschal season, till the Leavetaking of Pascha,** we replace "O come, let us worship" with the Paschal hymn, Christ is risen from the dead... (3x).]

And here follows the Psalm:

In the evening, Ps.142 (143), O Lord, hear my prayer...
In the morning, Ps.50 (51), Have mercy on me, O God, according to thy great mercy...

After the Psalm, the Reader concludes: Glory/Both now. And we continue with the Symbol of Faith (i.e. the Creed), followed by the Prayer >> p.t.o.

---

*) The abbreviation "Glory/Both now" refers to the oft repeated phrase, "Glory [be] to the Father, and (etc)", printed in full on the previous page.
**) According to an ancient tradition, from Pascha onwards we do not make full prostrations for the entire Fifty Days, till the Kneeling Prayers on the Sunday of Pentecost. (Note that in certain monastic traditions some of the common Paschal adjustments are restricted to Bright Week.)

The Symbol of Faith
- also known as The Creed -

I BELIEVE IN ONE GOD, the Father Almighty,
> Maker of heaven and earth,
> and of all things visible and invisible;

AND IN ONE LORD, JESUS CHRIST,
> the Only-Begotten Son of God,
> begotten of the Father before all ages;
> Light from Light, true God from true God,
> begotten, not made,
> one in essence with the Father,
> And through Whom all things were made;

Who, for us men and for our salvation, came down from
> the heavens, and was incarnate of the Holy Spirit and
> the Virgin Mary, and became man;
> And was also crucified for us, under Pontius Pilate,
> and suffered and was buried; And on the third day He
> rose again, in accordance with the Scriptures;
> And ascended into the heavens,
> and is seated at the right hand of the Father;

And He shall come again with glory
> to judge both the living and the dead,
> And His kingdom shall have no end;

AND IN THE HOLY SPIRIT, the Lord, the Giver of Life,
> Who proceeds from the Father,
> Who together with the Father and the Son
> is worshipped and glorified,
> Who spoke through the prophets;

AND IN ONE, HOLY, CATHOLIC AND APOSTOLIC CHURCH:
> I confess one Baptism for the remission of sins,
> I look for the resurrection of the dead,
> and the life of the age to come.

AMEN.

Then we recite the Prayer, as set out on the following pages:

p.116 Common Prayer with the Prayer Rope:
Basic Patterns and Alternatives

p.118 Between the Rounds of the Prayer Rope
- The Usual Order
- During the Paschal Season
- Hymns to the Theotokos *

p.120 Texts for the Prayer Rope:
I. The Basic Petitions
II. Intercessions by Name

---

*) 'Theotokos' is the main title for the Virgin Mary, which may be translated 'Birthgiver of God'. Currently, several renderings of this ancient term are in common use. See page 105 for some further notes.

COMMON PRAYER WITH THE PRAYER ROPE

In services with the Prayer, one person repeats the prayer aloud, while the others attend in silence. Usually, there will be a set number of rounds (all of the same length: most commonly 100 knots, sometimes 50) – with several of those present taking it in turns to say a round of the prayer, which is normally arranged beforehand. The prayer rope is also used for the additional petitions and intercessions.

Below an outline of two basic patterns in common use:

I.   BASIC PATTERN (texts on p.120)

    A   The Jesus Prayer, one or more rounds depending on the time set aside for the service.

    B   One round of the prayer rope, including:
        1. To the Saints, by name;
        2. To all the Saints;
        3. For the Church and the whole world.

    C   To the Theotokos, one full round.

    D   And again the Jesus Prayer, one round, ending with one or more petitions for the whole world.

II.   WITH INTERCESSIONS BY NAME (texts on p.121)

The basic order is the same as above. The intercessions are added to the commemoration of the Saints, in the same round of the prayer rope:

    (A, as above)

    B   One round of the prayer rope, including:
        1. To the Saints, by name;
        2. Intercessions for the living;
        3. Intercessions for the departed;
        4. For the Church and the whole world.

    (C/D, as above)

ALTERNATVE PATTERNS

The second pattern (II.) described above, is particularly suitable for common prayer - giving due space to the daily commemoration of the Saints (using a church calendar) and with ample room to remember people by name.

In some situations, the first pattern (I.) may be preferable – possibly including special commemoration of those Saints with whom we have a particular connection. Both practices have shown their value in the communities where these are the daily rule.

However, at certain times we may benefit from an even more simple rule – especially when we are on our own. Some ascetics simply concentrate on the Prayer as such, adding one round to the Theotokos towards the end (as the last or penultimate round). Another, time-honoured rule, adds to this the prayer to all the Saints, as follows:

The Jesus Prayer (a few rounds)
Lord Jesus Christ, Son of God, have mercy upon us.

To the Theotokos (one round)
Most-holy [Birthgiver of God], save us.

To All the Saints (one round)
All ye Saints, pray to God for us.

concluding with the following, recited once:

> Lord Jesus Christ, through the prayers of thy Saints, have mercy upon us, and upon thy (whole) world.
>
> Lord Jesus Christ, our God,
> have mercy upon us and save us.

Generally, the Fathers advise to decide upon the available time, and work out how many rounds of the prayer rope will fit comfortably (including accompanying prayers). They prefer a stable rule, which we can keep up at all times.

BETWEEN THE ROUNDS OF THE PRAYER ROPE

The Usual Order

Outside the Paschal season, whoever begins the Prayer, first says: Glory [be] to the Father, and to the Son, and to the Holy Spirit, both now and ever, and unto the ages of ages. Amen. – And then recites the Prayer.

Between the rounds of the prayer rope we include a short doxology (like between the kathismata of the Psalter) – as set out below:

☩

After every round of the prayer rope, we conclude:

Glory [be] to the Father, and to the Son, and to the Holy Spirit, both now and ever, and unto the ages of ages. Amen.

    Alleluia, alleluia, alleluia, glory to Thee, O God. (3x)

At this point, <u>after the last round</u> of the prayer rope, we continue with the hymns >> p.122 etc.

But if another round is to follow, we continue:

    Lord, have mercy. (3x) Glory [be] to the Father, and to the Son, and to the Holy Spirit –

If someone else will say the next round, that person completes the sentence (otherwise one says it all):

 – Both now and ever, and unto the ages of ages. Amen.
    (and the next round)

DURING THE PASCHAL SEASON

Instead of "Glory... (etc)" we begin the first round with the Paschal troparion, recited <u>once</u>: Christ is risen from the dead, trampling down death by death, and upon those in the tombs bestowing life.

Between the rounds we recite this <u>thrice</u> – but the third time, the first person says, "Christ is risen from the dead, trampling down death by death –" and the next one concludes: "– and upon those in the tombs bestowing life." – and continues with the Prayer.

Whoever says the last round concludes with the same troparion, recited <u>thrice</u> – after which we continue with the hymns, as usual >> p.122 etc.

HYMNS TO THE THEOTOKOS

At the beginning and the end of the prayer rope to the Theotokos, some also recite the following hymns:

At the beginning, after "Glory/Both now":

– REJOICE, O VIRGIN BIRTHGIVER OF GOD: MARY FULL OF GRACE, THE LORD IS WITH THEE. BLESS-ED ART THOU AMONG WOMEN, AND BLESS-ED IS THE FRUIT OF THY WOMB, FOR THOU HAST GIVEN BIRTH TO THE SAVIOUR OF OUR SOULS.

At the end, before the next "Glory":

– MEET IT IS IN VERY TRUTH, TO CALL THEE BLESS-ED, O BIRTHGIVER OF GOD, EVER-BLESS-ED AND ALL-PURE AND THE MOTHER OF OUR GOD. MORE HONOURABLE THAN THE CHERUBIM, AND PAST COMPARE MORE GLORIOUS THAN THE SERAPHIM, THOU WHO INVIOLATE DIDST BEAR GOD THE WORD: INDEED THE BIRTHGIVER OF GOD, THEE DO WE MAGNIFY.

I. THE BASIC PETITIONS

A. THE JESUS PRAYER, said on behalf of all, one or more rounds, depending on the available time – repeating:
Lord Jesus Christ, Son of God, have mercy upon us.

B. TO THE SAINTS & INTERCESSION - in the same round:
1) <u>To the Saints, by name</u>

Saint /Holy Father /Martyr /Prophet /... N, pray to God for us. – For each saint, repeat this a few times, ending:

Through the prayers of [Saint/... N,] Lord Jesus Christ, our God, have mercy upon us and save us.

Then may follow intercessions by name (see right), or else the following, repeated a few times:

2) <u>To All the Saints</u>

All ye Saints, pray to God for us. (repeat)

3) <u>For the Church and the whole world</u>

Lord Jesus Christ, by the prayers of thy Saints, have mercy upon us, and upon thy world. (once)

Lord Jesus Christ, our God, have mercy upon us, and upon thy (whole) world. (once, or repeat)

C. TO THE THEOTOKOS - one full round, repeating:
Most-holy [Birthgiver of God], save us.
(This prayer may be preceded and concluded with hymns to the Theotokos, as noted on the previous page.)

D. AND AGAIN, THE JESUS PRAYER, concluding with one or more petitions for the whole world:

Lord Jesus Christ, Son of God, have mercy upon us. (repeat)

Lord Jesus Christ, our God, have mercy upon us, and upon thy (whole) world. (once, or repeat a few times)

Ending with: **Lord Jesus Christ, our God, have mercy upon us and save us.**

II. INTERCESSIONS BY NAME

The prayer rope to the Saints (part B) can be combined with intercessions by name, as follows:

1) <u>To the Saints, by name</u> (see left, as noted)

2) <u>Intercessions, for the living</u>:
We start with naming those we wish to pray for (e.g. our bishop, spiritual father, absent members of our household, and anyone dear to us or in special need):
Lord Jesus Christ, have mercy upon thy servant(s) [N.]

Having named one or more people, we then repeat the general petition, a few times after each set of names:
Lord Jesus Christ, have mercy upon thy servant(s).

Having prayed for all those named, we conclude with:
Lord Jesus Christ, have mercy upon all those who have asked us, unworthy as we are, to pray for them (and grant them all their petitions that are unto salvation).

3) <u>For the departed</u>:
As for the living, we first name those we pray for:
Lord Jesus Christ, give rest to
thy (newly) departed servant(s) [N.]

Then we repeat the general petition:
Lord Jesus Christ, give rest to thy servant(s).

And we conclude with:
Lord Jesus Christ, give rest to thy departed servants where the light of thy countenance watches over them.

4) <u>Finally, for the Church and the whole world:</u>
Lord Jesus Christ, have mercy upon us,
and upon thy (whole) world. (repeat a few times)

Then we continue with the prayers to the Theotokos etc (part C/D, see left).

After the Prayer we chant the GREAT DOXOLOGY - in some places only on the eve of the Liturgy, and in the mornings

Introduced by Deacon/Priest (or, in some traditions, by Choir/Chanter): Glory [be] to Thee, Who hast shown forth the Light. – Choir/Chanter:

- Glory [be] to God in the Highest, and on earth peace, good-will towards men. We hymn Thee, we bless Thee, we worship Thee, we glorify Thee, we give thanks unto Thee for thy great glory: O Lord King, Heavenly God, Father Almighty; O Lord, Only-begotten Son, Jesus Christ; and Thou, O Holy Spirit.

O Lord God, Lamb of God, Son of the Father, that takest away the sin of the world, have mercy upon us; Thou that takest away the sins of the world, receive our prayer, Thou that sittest at the Right hand of the Father, and have mercy upon us. For Thou only art Holy, Thou only art the Lord, O Jesus Christ, to the glory of God the Father, Amen.

Every day will I bless Thee, and praise thy Name for ever, yea, for ever and ever, Amen. Vouchsafe, O Lord, to keep us this day without sin. Bless-ed art Thou, O Lord, God of our Fathers, and praised and glorified be thy Name unto the ages, Amen. Let thy mercy, O Lord, be upon us, even as we have hoped in Thee.

Bless-ed art Thou, O Lord, teach me thy statutes. (3x)

O Lord, Thou hast been our refuge from generation to generation. I said: O Lord, have mercy upon me; heal my soul, for I have sinned against Thee. O Lord, unto Thee have I fled for refuge: teach me to do thy will, for Thou art my God. For with Thee is the Fount of Life, in thy Light shall we see Light. O continue thy mercy on them that know Thee.

Holy God, Holy and Strong, Holy and Immortal, have mercy upon us. (3x).

Glory [be] to the Father, and to the Son, and to the Holy Spirit, both now and ever, and unto the ages of ages. Amen.   – Holy and Immortal, have mercy upon us.

(And we repeat:) Holy God, Holy and Strong, Holy and Immortal, have mercy upon us.

Instead, on other evenings, we may chant the NINTH ODE (also known as the Magnificat, Lk. 1:46-55):

Introduced by Deacon/Priest: **Let us honour in hymns and magnify the Birthgiver of God and Mother of the Light.**

– My soul does magnify the Lord, and my spirit has rejoiced in God my Saviour.

Refrain, repeated after each verse:

– More honourable than the Cherubim, and past compare more glorious than the Seraphim, thou who inviolate didst bear God the Word: indeed the Birthgiver of God, thee do we magnify.

For He has looked upon the humbleness of His handmaid; for behold, from henceforth all generations shall call me bless-ed.   Refrain: – More honourable …

For the Mighty One has done great things to me, and holy is His name; and His mercy is on them that fear Him, from generation to generation.

Same Refrain: – More honourable than the Cherubim, and past compare more glorious than the Seraphim, thou who inviolate didst bear God the Word: indeed the Birthgiver of God, thee do we magnify.

He has wrought strength with His arm, He has scattered the proud in the imagination of their heart.

Refrain: – More honourable ...

He has brought down the mighty from their thrones, and the humble ones has he exalted; He has filled the hungry with good things, and the rich He has sent empty away.   Refrain: – More honourable ...

He has holpen His servant Israel in remembrance of His mercy, as He spake to our fathers, to Abraham and his seed for ever.   Refrain: – More honourable ...

Then the Troparia

We follow the usual pattern (as at the end of Daily Vespers or the beginning of Matins) depending on the weekday and/or feasts and periods of the Liturgical Year. Except on the Great Feasts, one may also add the apolytikion of the local church or chapel(s).

Here, by means of example, the Apolytikion for All Saints with the corresponding Theotokion of the Resurrection. Instead, we may chant to the Theotokos, as given below:

Apolytikion for All Saints (tone 4)

- Adorned with the blood of thy Martyrs in all the world, as with purple and fine linen, thy Church, O Christ God, through them cries out to Thee: Send down Thy compassions upon Thy people, unto Thy commonwealth grant peace, and unto our souls the great mercy.

Glory... / Both now...

Theotokion of the Resurrection (same tone)

- The mystery hidden from all ages, and unknown even to the angels, was made manifest to those on earth through thee, O Birthgiver of God: God took flesh in a union without confusion, and for our sake willingly accepted the Cross; thereby He resurrected the first-formed man, and saved our souls from death.

INSTEAD of the troparia, we may chant to the Theotokos (as at the end of Vespers in a Sunday Vigil):

- Rejoice, O Virgin Birthgiver of God: Mary full of grace, the Lord is with thee. Bless-ed art thou among women, and bless-ed is the fruit of thy womb, for thou hast given birth to the Saviour of our souls. (3x)

BUT IN THE PASCHAL SEASON instead of the usual troparia, we chant the Paschal Troparion (or else, if available, the appointed troparia from the Pentecostarion):

- Christ is risen from the dead, trampling down death by death, and upon those in the tombs bestowing life. (3x)

Followed by the Dismissal

[Priest: Most-holy Birthgiver of God, save us.]

Reader: More honourable than the Cherubim, and past compare more glorious than the Seraphim, thou who inviolate didst bear God the Word: indeed the Birthgiver of God, thee do we magnify.

[Priest: Glory to Thee, O Christ, our God and our hope, glory to Thee.]

Glory [be] to the Father, and to the Son, and to the Holy Spirit, both now and ever, and unto the ages of ages. Amen.

Lord, have mercy. (3x)

[If a Priest be present: Father, give the blessing.
Priest: May ... Christ our true God .... / Reader: Amen.
Otherwise: Through the prayers of our holy Fathers, Lord Jesus Christ, our God, have mercy upon us. Amen.]

At certain times, here may follow one final hymn, In the Evening, to the Theotokos:

– UNDER THY COMPASSION DO WE TAKE REFUGE, O THEOTOKOS: DESPISE NOT OUR SUPPLICATIONS IN THE MIDST OF TROUBLE, BUT FROM PERILS DELIVER US, O THOU WHO ALONE ART PURE AND BLESS-ED. [And in some traditions we conclude this ancient hymn with: MOST HOLY THEOTOKOS, SAVE US.]

Instead, on Wednesday and Friday we may chant the following, both on the eve and in the morning:

– BEFORE THY CROSS WE BOW DOWN, O MASTER, AND THY HOLY RESURRECTION WE GLORIFY. (3x)

After the hymn, the Priest (or else the Reader) concludes: Through the prayers of our holy Fathers, Lord Jesus Christ, our God, have mercy upon us. / Reader: Amen.

Conclusion for All Services in the Paschal Season

During the Paschal season – till the Leavetaking on the 40th day – after the blessing by the Priest "May..." (or "Through the prayers", if without a Priest) we do not chant the final hymns mentioned above, but <u>instead, every service</u> is simply concluded with the Paschal ending:

– AND HE GAVE US LIFE ETERNAL,

  LET US VENERATE HIS RESURRECTION ON THE THIRD DAY.

[Note: In some places, the Paschal ending is done in a different way – in which case we may follow local usage.]

Additional Troparia & Personal Notes